Seeds of an Entrepreneur

Simple Guide to Change your Habits, Start your Business and Live a Life of Success

By Rachael L. Thompson

Introduction

I want to thank you for purchasing the book, "Seeds of an Entrepreneur".

Dear Aspiring Entrepreneur,

Likely you looked at this book because you are yearning for a happier, more fulfilling, and more successful life. Maybe you are sick of working for someone else, you're tired of the 9-5 grind, you want to do work you are passionate about, you want more free time to spend with loved ones, or you can feel your life slipping away and want to take action to turn things around. So many of us feel like this but are scared and unsure how to change things.

You are not alone if you feel called to get out of your comfort zone but feel stuck and do not know how to even begin this journey. There are plenty of success stories of those who "made it" but people often develop a mindset that this type of successful life is only for others and is not an option for themselves. These successful people must be different. They must have been smarter, wealthier, better at business, had more connections, so on. The truth is that many people with the same amount of education, intelligence, money, business knowledge and connections as you have completely changed their lives and found the happiness they were chasing.

This book will help take you from a point of wanting a better life to a point of taking action to pursue this. It is not a business basics book. You will not get the nuts and bolts of starting a business, but this will give you the tools to begin to plan how you can take your strengths and passions and turn them into a profitable business. Becoming an entrepreneur is more than just learning about business, and this book will help you develop a lifestyle and mindset that will set you up for success.

Each chapter has "Action Steps" to take. You can read through the book first and then go back to take action or you can take the suggested steps at the end of each chapter as you read along. No matter your approach, the important thing is that you start to take some action. Do not worry about making everything perfect or making the "right" decisions as this will only slow you down. At this stage, you can always go back and make changes. Remember that you are in the exciting first phase of brainstorming what you truly want to do and how you can become successful doing it. Trust in yourself and enjoy the process of developing the life and career you desire.

Table of Contents

Chapter 1: Discover What You Should Be Doing Today

There can always be more to life but you have to decide what that "more" is for you. What are you missing? What would make you happy? To figure out the right path, you must be very honest with yourself. Your road to success will not look like anyone else's. Often people look to other's for inspiration, but instead feel the need to mimic what these people did instead of figuring out what works best for them. After Steve Job's biography came out many were inspired to replicate his success. His strategies lead to huge success, but when replicated would not work for many others. It simply would not be a fit with their values, personality, work-ethic, etc. To figure out what your best path is you must examine your strengths, weaknesses, values, and goals. Let's look at Maggie's case study

Maggie was a passionate cook. She aspired to open up her own restaurant. She built a brand for herself through catering but spent years yearning for that bricks and mortar location she could call home. As much as Maggie loved cooking, she equally disliked many other business aspects. The business plan and financial projections prevented her from taking those next steps. Maggie eventually found a business partner who was a great marketer and had experience in managing and finance. Together, they opened a restaurant. Maggie is the head chef, created and updates the menu, and manages the kitchen staff. Her partner focuses on the marketing and financial aspects of the business. It is the perfect team. If Maggie had tried to run the restaurant all by herself, she may have ended miserable or very stressed out. She knew her strengths and weaknesses and found a balance that allowed her to pursue her passion.

If you are going to make a career out of your passions you must become crystal clear on what your passions are. What will make you happy and what will drain you? This is not to say that you will never have to do something that challenges you. Often challenges help get you to your end goal. They arise unexpectedly and must be overcome. This is normal and happens to every new entrepreneur.

There is a difference between facing minor challenges periodically and being challenged daily in a negative way. Through honest introspection you will be able to explore what factors will set you up for success and fulfillment and what factors will contribute to unhappiness and unwanted stress. Think about what jobs you liked the most and why. Think about what aspects in your current job you like and dislike and why. If you could make one hobby a job, what would that be and why. Dig deeper and deeper and continue to ask yourself why. The more crystal clear you are in this process, the more likely you will set yourself up for long-term happiness and success. Think, if you embark on a venture that is a complete failure, would you at least enjoy the process? If the answer is no, then you need to re-examine what you want to pursue.

Note the following example to get insight into what this self-exploration process looks like. Let's say that you love fashion and want to somehow get into this industry. A similar Q&A brainstorming session may occur:

What about fashion do I like?
Shopping. Picking out outfits and finding the perfect accessories to complete it.

What about this is exciting for me?
Expressing my creativity, working towards an end goal, and getting instant gratification when that outfit is complete.

What do I value most in life?
Money, social acceptance, and making own schedule.

What are my strengths?

People skills, creativity, thinking outside the box, lots of energy.

What are my weaknesses?
Not great at sales-feel pushy. Do not like monotonous tasks. Organization. Writing and computer oriented tasks.

Based on these answers, we can probably determine that the person in this example should not be an online fashion blogger, run an online store, and will likely need assistance with mundane, organizational tasks. She would also not do well with opening her own store, as this will hinder her being able to make her own schedule and she does not like sales. She would probably be an excellent stylist, as long as she has some assistance with the mundane tasks. She will likely excel at meeting new people and finding unique outfits. We could also assume that although she wants to make her own schedule, she does not mind working long hours. She values money and would be willing to sacrifice time for money. She also values social acceptance and would be willing to work hard for those "right" clients.

Now it is time to put this brainstorming process into action.

Action Steps:

1)Make a list of your values. (Time, freedom, money, etc.)
2)Ask yourself self-exploring questions. The more the better: What do you want out of your perfect career? What things would you excel at? What things are you not good at? What do you like? What do you hate? Go as deep as you can with all of these.

These two steps are to just get you thinking about what would be the best career options for you. Do not get bogged down with logistics yet. There will be time later to work through these. This first step is to make sure that your career ideas align with your value system. The more ideas you can generate the better; you will learn later that there has to be a market for your concepts. If you come out of this exercise with three concrete ideas, then you can figure out which idea has the most chance for success. Don't be afraid to think outside of the box and include things you may have told yourself are impossible.

Chapter 2: How Do You Get Into a Pool? Jumpers vs. Inchers

There is a shift in mindset that occurs when one begins an entrepreneurial journey. This shift takes a person from thinking that only others can be entrepreneurs to eventually believing he or she can be a successful business owner. The first step in this shift is simply believing that it is possible and seeing oneself, one's strengths, and one's gifts as possible assets.

This journey can be filled with feelings of nervousness and the sense of being overwhelmed as well as feelings of excitement. Some jump right in while others take years to reach the point when they feel they are ready to start something of their own. Many factors play a role in this, including personality type, thinking patterns, current situations, and perception. The type of person who tends to jump right in to the entrepreneur pool inclines to be one who views a new venture as exciting and likes change, while someone who values security and is filled with anxiety is likely to take much longer and will require much more self-work to feel comfortable taking risks.

This is not to say that someone who eases into something is in a worse position. In fact, these often are the same people who will embark only on a journey they feel confident will succeed while someone who jumps right in may experience more failures until they reach their success. Knowing what type of personality you have is crucial to determine what you will need to focus on in your personal journey.

Action Steps:

Take a few moments now to write down all of the thoughts and feelings that arise when you think about starting your own business. Evaluate underlying themes in these responses and decide if you are a "jumper" or an "incher".

If you are Type I (Pool Jumper):

If you are excited and want to start this minute then it will be important that you begin to do research, as we will discuss in a later chapter, and be cautious that you do not jump into anything without setting yourself up for success first.

Write down an action plan for the next three months. What steps must you take to set yourself up for success? If you are unsure, the first step would be to get a business startup book in your field, take a course or find a mentor. There is a lot of free information on the internet, with a plethora of blogs, YouTube tutorials and forums. Do not, however, underestimate the immense value you can gain from investing in online courses, coaching and books.

If you are Type II (Pool Incher):

If you find that you are feeling overwhelmed, anxious, and unsure then find the main source of these negative thoughts and feelings. For some, internal factors, such as lack of confidence or fear, are their biggest obstacles, while others are faced with external concerns, such as finances. The source of your anxiety will provide the answer to how you will overcome it.

If you simply do not know where to start when planning for your business, find a book, course, or mentor who can break down the next steps for you. With so many courses online, you do not have to go back to college. You can find business 101 resources for free or at a much lower cost than enrolling in classes.

Make a plan for the next three to six months to help break down the steps and set realistic goals for yourself.

One of the biggest sources for concern is finances. Obtaining funding to start a business and giving up the security of a nine to five job can be huge causes of uncertainty. If financing is a source of stress, brainstorm ways to start small that do not require loans or investors while you also research various types of financing.

If quitting your current job is a concern you will need to get a deep understanding of your current financial situation and how much money you need to make to cover all of your expenses. You essentially have two options:

1) Keep your current job and work on your business on the side.

2) Find a side job to cover your expenses to free up time to work on your business.

Break both options down simply and concretely. For example, if you need $3000 a month to cover all of your expenses then you will need to make approximately $100 a day. How will you be able to execute this? Could you get a part-time job to make this money? If you want to keep your current job figure out how much time each day or week you can dedicate towards your new business. If you can only work an hour a day, in six months you would have worked almost 200 hours on your business.

Follow this same process for anything else that overwhelms you. Figure out how you will overcome these obstacles to enable you to take action.

Chapter 3: Number One Factor of Success vs. Failure

Now that you have brainstormed ideas, begin to do some research in the field you want to enter. Is there a need that is not being met? Is there a market for the product or service you want to provide? How will you meet the need for the demand in a different way?

Do not get sucked into trying to replicate how others have done things but rather begin to think about how your talents will be able to fulfill a demand in an entirely new way. Check out others who are doing something similar and explore what they are doing. Use this insight to brainstorm about how you can enter this field. Look for trends. Go to the location (if there is one) of your competitors, the websites, and the social media platforms. Read reviews of products or services similar to what you want to do. Look at the services your competitors provide and at what prices. This investigating will help you learn which one of your ideas may be profitable.

Let's look at a successful vs. a non-successful venture to help you understand the importance of researching your ideas.

Person A has been brewing his own beer for a few years and all of his friends and family tell him he should sell his beverages. He decides to take the leap and get a loan to open up his own brewery. He finds a good price on an old building that is big enough for his large machinery. Six months and $250,000 later he opens the doors. He quickly finds that it is a challenge to bring enough customers in to cover his monthly bills. He also finds that he has a few regulars but he fails to have repeat customers on a consistent basis. His dream soon becomes a nightmare as he struggles to pay his bills, racks up more debt and spends more and more time away from his friends and family trying to keep his business afloat.

Person B was a manager of bars and restaurants for years while saving up enough money to start his own bar. He was fairly connected in the industry and stayed informed on trends. He had been hearing a lot about Prohibition style bars and thought is sounded like an interesting concept. Upon further research he finds one such bar in his own city. He goes there and hangs out, both during the week and on the weekend. He talks to customers, asking them how often they come and what draws them to this place. He also finds reviews online and reads through all of the good and bad remarks. He travels to visit friends in different cities, and checks out similar style bars in each of these different cities. He finds that in his city, people mainly go to the Prohibition bar because of the location and they like that they can smoke cigars. Consistent complaints from customers are about the lack of creative, signature drinks and the lackluster design of the bar. He sees that in other cities, the bars had the bartenders dress in 1920's attire, the décor is appropriate for the Prohibition era and they sell unique craft cocktails. After his research, he hunts for a bar space in a similar location to the bar in his city. Once he finds a possible location he hangs out at bars and restaurants nearby to scope out the typical clientele. This confirms it would be a high-traffic location with his target demographic. He leases the space and designs the bar with a 1920's décor, a cigar room and develops a menu with unique signature cocktails. Word soon spreads about his bar and he has a steady stream of customers. It is a success.

In both of these stories, the owners were passionate, but they experienced drastically different outcomes. So why was one successful while the other struggled? The number one reason is that Person A opened his business for himself while Person B opened it for his customers. Person A based his concept solely on what he wanted and what his friends and family encouraged him to do. He picked a location that was affordable and spacious but did zero research on the traffic and customer demographic in that area. He had an "if you build it, they will come" attitude. Person B was open to all different concepts and made his choices based on trends. He did thorough research on what customers wanted and designed a bar to meet their needs. He searched for locations based on the current traffic of his target demographic. If Person A had followed the same approach as Person B did, he could have found success with his brewery.

Many fear failure when they hear the high statistics of businesses that fail within the first several years. There are, however, ways to set yourself up for a higher chance of success. When one simply does something because they enjoy doing it, it is like throwing spaghetti at the wall. It could stick or plummet. The more research one does and the more flexibility one has to alter his or her original plan to fit the needs of the target customer, the more confidence one can have embarking on the business venture. You should have a list of ideas you would like to pursue. Now is the time to research each one of your ideas and begin to plan how you will turn your ideas and passions into a business.

Action Steps: Develop your research plan. Brainstorm the following and go to websites, blogs, social media platforms and locations of competitors and/or those who are doing something similar to what you want to do to find answers.

1) Google your ideas to begin to see if there is a market and need for what you want to do. Are people already doing this or something similar?

2) Who are your customers (age, gender, salary, likes/dislikes, interests)?

3) What are your competitors doing to meet their customers' needs?

4) Read reviews of similar services or products. In these reviews, look for what people loved and what they did not like. You can go to Amazon and look for products, books, videos that are similar the niche you want to target.

5) What needs are still not being met by other businesses?

6) What would be the best location or online platform for your target population?

7) How can you reach and market to your target population to help them? Social media? YouTube? Blogging? Referrals? Advertising?

Chapter 4: Get Inspired Every Day

Those who are successful grow and learn every single day. After high school or college many simply stop learning. They may learn what they need to for a particular job or to complete a task, but they do not take initiative to continue learning for the learning's sake. This is a must if you want to be a successful entrepreneur and the best time to start is now. It is not as daunting as it may first appear if you simply dedicate yourself to learning one new thing each day. If you find that you hate learning the information that applies to your entrepreneurial goal then it would be wise to seriously re-evaluate what you want to do.

It is exceptionally easy to find free information from those who have done exactly what you want to do. Search this out. Read blogs and books. Joins email lists. Subscribe to YouTube channels. Read stories of people who started in a similar, or worse-off, position as you and are now successful. You can get plenty of ideas and inspiration from these stories.

Learn from other's successes as well as failures. Do not make the same mistakes that someone before you has already made. Through this process you can even learn new business opportunities that you never knew existed. You may develop a completely different approach to your business after learning about new options.

Think of how you can incorporate learning and inspiration into your everyday life. You can get audible books from the library, download books or find podcasts on iTunes to listen to in the car, while you are walking or exercising, and performing daily tasks, like cooking or cleaning. Instead of spending time on social media, spend time reading inspirational blogs. Instead of watching TV, watch YouTube videos. There are endless ways to incorporate learning into your daily tasks.

Each new phase of you entrepreneur journey will begin with learning. After you decide on an idea you want to pursue you will need to get information on business basics. These basics may include, developing a business plan, choosing a business structure, financial projections, marketing plan, obtaining funding, and branding.

After you understand general business basics you will have to learn specifically how to execute particular tasks. For example, in social media marketing you will have to learn how to set up a business Facebook account, how to draw customers to it, what and how to post, etc. This list is not meant to be overwhelming, rather it is just meant to showcase that each stage of a business starts with learning.

Nobody is born with knowledge on how to run a successful business. It only comes from learning and taking action. Learn and take action on one thing at a time. What seems overwhelming now will soon appear much more feasible.

Action Steps:
1) Decide what the next step will be in your journey and how you will gain the knowledge needed to prepare yourself to take the next step.
2) Find three entrepreneurs who inspire you. Look on Google, YouTube, read blogs or ask fellow entrepreneurs who they follow. Sign up for each of their email lists and see if they have any Facebook groups or forums you can join. Begin to read about their journey.

Important Note*** Make sure to look for successful people to inspire you but do not compare yourself or try to change who you are to be like them. Every single person has their own values, work-ethic and journey. Along with finding highly successful influencers, try to also follow those who are just a few steps ahead of you in their entrepreneur journey. Their steps will be easier to relate to than someone who has been working for 10, 15 or 30+ years.

Chapter 5: Find the Support that You Need

One of the biggest challenges new entrepreneurs face is lack of support. Often people sit and think about all of their dreams for years before uttering a single word of them to a family member or friend. And then when that person finally musters the courage to tell those close to them, it can be met with doubt, lack of understanding, and a list of all the reasons it is a bad idea.

The other end of the spectrum is the overly encouraging support system. The family who tells you every idea sounds wonderful and you will surely succeed at anything you put your mind to. It is frankly hard to find the best balance of support and realistic advice when it comes to gaining support from those in your current social circle. Those who are not entrepreneurs have a very difficult time understanding the lifestyle, mindset, challenges and decisions you must make.

Although it can be difficult to find support, it is just as hard to be a one-man-show. Finding a group of like-minded individuals who can provide encouragement, advice and accountability will help your business pursuits and your overall well-being. But how does one find such a support system?

The term mastermind group is commonly used in the entrepreneurial world. All this means is a group of success driven, motivated individuals who share a common goal and get together, either on a call, in person, or over the internet, to share ideas, encourage each other and hold one another accountable. The importance of this group is to help the members stay on track and get the support that is vital for success.

For someone who is just beginning in their journey, this may seem quite intimidating, and you may think that you need a certain level of success before looking into such a support system. The contrary is actually the case. If you had a small leak in your roof and a neighbor offered to help fix it, would you take him up on the offer or wait until it turned into a huge leak and flooded your house? You probably would want to get it fixed while it was still small, easy to manage and before it caused any damage. The same can be applied to business. People often delay seeking help or advice until they have a problem but if you get support early you can prevent many problems and set your business up for success.

Finding groups can be less intimidating than it first seems. Try to find groups that have people who are at the same level as you and also some who have already learned the hard lessons of entrepreneurship and can help guide you. You can look for aspiring entrepreneur groups online or in your local neighborhood. Explore Meetups (www.meetup.com) in your city for aspiring or new entrepreneurs. If there are no options for in-person groups there will always be support online. Begin to look at different forums. You can begin on platforms like Quora (www.quora.com) or Reddit (www.reddit.com) or look for specific platforms related to your goals. Here you are able to ask questions or simply read through other's questions and answers that relate to topics you are interested in. There are also tons of Facebook groups available to join. Do not be reluctant to join groups that are labeled "closed". Often if you request to join, they will accept your request. Also, do not feel pressured to join online groups and participate immediately. You can scope several out and explore the best fit before engaging. Through online groups, members will often form outside mastermind groups, kind of like study groups, where they talk periodically via skype, google hangout or on conference calls. You can keep an eye out for these opportunities or, as you become more comfortable, look into forming one yourself.

Action Steps: Look for one to three free or low cost support groups to join. These can be local meet-ups in your city or town or online groups on Facebook, Reddit, Quora and other forums. Make sure that these groups consist of members that are at a similar point, such as entrepreneurs in the planning or beginning stages.

Chapter 6: Take Action TODAY

As stated throughout the book, action is the key to success. You will never think your way to success but you can act your way to success. The best way to take action is to set goals for yourself and develop a plan to get to the next stage in your journey.

Your overall plan can easily be managed by developing small goals and steps. You can begin today, at this very moment, to work towards the life and career of your dreams. It is the perfect time to start setting and working towards small goals. This is a habit that will help you become as efficient and effective as possible. Do not feel that you need to know all of the right goals to set at this time. There is no such thing as "right" or "wrong" goals. The important part is that you set goals you are able to take action on immediately. Accomplishing each small goal will give you the motivation to continue along your journey and you will gain momentum and confidence through this process. Let's explore a simple way to tackle goal setting and action planning.

When making goals, keep the acronym SMART in mind. This will guide you in setting specific and actionable goals. This SMART goal guide will help break down huge, overwhelming goals into small ones that you can easily accomplish. Try to break every goal down to make sure that it is as SMART as possible, using the following guide.

SMART GOALS:
S: Specific - The goal is as detailed and clear as possible.
M: Measurable - The goal can be measured numerically
A: Attainable & Actionable - You will be able to achieve this goal and take action on it today.
R: Relevant & Realistic - The goal is relevant to your overall plan and will be realistic for you to accomplish.
T: Time-bound - The goal has a start and end time that it must be accomplished by.

Now let's look at a broad (bad) goal compared to a SMART goal.

Example of bad goal: Learn more about business.

Example of a SMART goal: Read 1 business book (Specific and Measurable) by the end of this week (Time-Bound). It is also something that you can take action on and is relevant to your over-arching goal. Only you will know if it is attainable and realistic for you.

The next step is to break down the SMART goal into actionable steps and plan how you will accomplish this goal. If you are going to buy a business book then the first step may be to research books by looking on Amazon and reading book descriptions and reviews. The second step would be placing an order for the book you decide on. The third step would be to set time aside to read this book, perhaps for an hour each evening. Goals, no matter how great, will not mean anything unless you have a clear plan of how you will work towards accomplishing them.

Below are three questions you can answer to help figure out what the next goal will be in your journey.

1)What is your final goal? Or, if you are unsure, what is your goal for the next month?

2)What are the big steps to get to this goal?

3)What is one goal that you can set today?

Look at the following example to get some ideas of where to start:

1)   What is your final goal? Or, if you are unsure, what is your goal for the next month?

To open a hair salon

2)What are the big steps to get to this goal?

   1.Learn business basics

   2.Figure out financing

3.Develop business model
4.Find location

3)What is one goal that you can set today?

This person was clear that she wanted to open a salon and set up some basic goals she thought would lead her to this. Throughout her journey, these goals will likely change and become more concrete and detailed but this is an excellent starting point. In this process she figured out that the goal she could accomplish today was to sign up for a business course. After she has found a good course, she can make additional SMART goals to help her complete the business course and apply what she has learned.

Action Step: Answer the above three questions for yourself. For each larger goal, think of ways to break it down into smaller, actionable goals and pick a place to start. Once this is done, set a goal to work on today. Make sure that it is as SMART as possible and is accompanied with a realistic plan to execute it. Once this goal is accomplished, immediately set the next goal for yourself.

This SMART goal process can, and should, be applied to any of the earlier "Action Steps" listed in previous chapters. If you have been working on these action steps, go back now and make sure all of your goals and plans are SMART.

Conclusion

Turning your passion into a career can be simultaneously exciting and terrifying. You deserve a lot credit for purchasing a book about pursuing a better, more fulfilling life. Many just dream about it but never take that first step. You have taken that step and have begun your journey. You can now decide what tools you wish to take from this book and apply them to your life. Remember to take everything one step at a time, to brainstorm, be honest and introspective, to search out support and education, to start small and break everything down, and to view this as an exciting new chapter in your journey to success. My hope is that this book has encouraged a little more clarity, gotten your wheels turning and prepared you to take action to work towards the life you know that you deserve.

Finally, if you enjoyed this book, then I'd like to ask you for a favor, would you be kind enough to leave a review for this book on Amazon? It'd be greatly appreciated!

About the Author

I sat on the trolley every morning and evening commuting to and from work. To a job that required a Master's degree. A job that took six years in school with a 4.0 GPA and six months after graduating with my M.A. to get. A job that I moved and bought a house for and was very excited to begin. A job that quickly sucked the life out of me, yet I continued to work at for over four years. So, for over four years, I sat on that trolley and looked at the fellow commuters. They all looked miserable. I would sit there every day thinking I do not want to be riding on this trolley for the remainder of my working years. Nevertheless, I sat there year after year and never made a change. Often my co-worker and I would talk about the businesses we would want to open and how fun it would be to live a life other than one where we dreaded work each day. It always seemed like a nice dream to fantasize about but one that never seemed in reach. I remember telling my supervisor in grad school I just wanted a job I looked forward to working each day and she scoffed at the seemingly naïve comment. It seemed I always had this feeling there was more out there but I did not know what it was.

It was not until I moved to a new city that a shift began. I moved for a new, happy life but soon fell back into old routines, applying for jobs I was not passionate about for salaries far beneath what I wanted. A simple discussion with my boyfriend, in which he stated there should be more pet stores in our dog-friendly area, prompted my mind shift. I love animals. I had money from selling my house and I could be the one to open this pet store!

I began to explore opening a bricks and mortar pet boutique. The neighborhood I lived in was full of dogs and I was confident it would be a success. I went to the library and started to search for books about business. They all seemed so boring and dry, until I found one that drew me in. Through reading this book, I learned that people from all walks of life, with different passions, have been successful opening their own businesses. This gave me a boost of confidence.

I found a local non-profit that offered business classes for those interested in starting their own businesses (www.score.org). I went through a 6 week course and was excited about continuing on this journey. To get experience in management, I became a manager at a coffee shop and also a dog walker while I continued to plan and look for store locations. I found out quickly, that I did not like managing. I was always on call. I remember taking a weekend trip and getting 5 calls on the way up from employees. This made me begin to question what it would be like if I opened up my own place. It made me a little uneasy to think about not having the freedom to enjoy a weekend away when I wanted. While this was happening, I was also not having any luck finding a location for a store in my area. In talking with my business mentor, I decided it would be a good idea to look into starting an online store while I continued to look for locations. I began to research this a bit further and realized it would be feasible. I had to, however, make an entirely new business plan. I began this process planning for a physical location but online was a new beast.

My online pet boutique was up and running within a few months of me making this decision. It is not initially easy to drive traffic to an online business but I began to see the potential of having a business based online. There was freedom in this. I could work from anywhere and make my own schedule. Every single day, I read tons of information, watched YouTube videos instead of TV, and listened to business podcasts in the car, instead of the radio. I also began a personal journey that involved intense work on my anxieties and mindset. I learned about manifesting and subconscious reprogramming, and applied the techniques. I became very honest with myself about what I truly wanted, and what personal traits and thoughts were holding me back from this. In the course of a year, I completely transformed.

I loved to tell my friends and family all the things I was learning and applying. I had some hiccups with my online pet boutique, due to manufacturer issues, and during this time re-evaluated what I truly wanted to do. Selling adorable animal products is fun but I wanted something more. Many online entrepreneurs have several businesses and I began to ponder what I could do next. I kept hearing about people fulfilling their "life purpose" and contemplated what that would look like for me. With my background in Psychology and Counseling, I felt compelled to help others. What a waste it would be for me to spend hours every day learning and developing all of these business and self-improvement techniques and not share them with anyone. Then I received a sign.

I was doing dishes, binge watching YouTube videos, when a video came on about writing and publishing books. I have always loved to write. As I sat down and watched the video and I was filled with excitement. I then searched for more free information online. I found Facebook groups where I learned from others doing this. I purchased several courses before beginning on this adventure. Everything about it just felt right. I can help others, use my formal background and education in Psychology, all my experience in starting and running a business, and do something I felt passionate about.

I understand that becoming an entrepreneur is about overcoming internal barriers as much as it is overcoming external barriers. My goal is to teach others how to overcome both. I share this long journey of mine to let you know it is not always a simple and straight road to success, but with the right tools and mindset you can get there. I hope to provide much more information with you on your road to success. Please reach out by signing up to my email list and shooting me a message about your current situation, triumphs, and struggles.